'Kate writes from the p _ where the Human meets the Divine. Her poems offer liberation, wisdom and authentic, gritty, truthful reminders of who we truly are - and how to remember this right in the middle of the beautiful mess and wonder of life as it unfolds. We are grateful to know Kate to know that her poetry is out there in the world, blessing - and kissing the Divine in - each reader.' **Robert and Hollie Holden**
**(www.everydaymiracles.love)**

'Katey's lovely words touched me so deeply that I was in tears reading them. Her poems are open, raw, honest, wise and funny too. And often all those things at once! I know what I will be getting everyone for their next birthday: this is an absolute amazing must read!' - **Shanti Schiks, Author of 'Elfin' (about love, loss and the power of yourself) and 'De kracht van zelfliefde' (The power of self love) and TED-X speaker of the same name (www.shantischiks.nl)**

'I have known Kate for more than 10 years and we have been each other's teacher and student on many occasions. Her dedication to always be truthful to herself and other people can sometimes be a bit confrontational but heart-warming and opening at the same time. She is committed to be real and authentic and wishes that for everybody else who is open to learn. Her Connection Experiments are amazing! Original, inspiring and a must for those wanting to learn about themselves and their environment. What Love Told Me gives you a glimpse of what she is in real life! If you want the real experience, connect with her in person! You will not regret it!' **Robbert Nuis, Author of the eBook 'Wake Up' (www.conscious-living-coaching.com)**

Kate has a way of wrapping you up and taking you on a journey of emotion, and her stories do exactly that! They are honest, powerful and beautiful in equal parts'. **Jayne Ashby, The Alternative (www.the-alternative.co.uk)**

'Kate's words have a way of cutting deep into your soul; it's as though she's walking in my shoes. Some of her poems I've read over and over again. There's a deep resonance in my heart, like I've been jolted awake and given a second chance at life. This collection will ignite you in ways that you may not logically understand.' **Michelle Catanach (www.uncaged.online)**

# WHAT LOVE TOLD ME

A collection of poetry to bring you back home

Written by Katey Roberts

For Me, for You, For Them:
As a constant reminder to BE Love.

'WHEN WE
EMBRACE OUR
HUMANITY, WE
EXPERIENCE
OUR DIVINITY'

- Hollie Holden

# A MESSAGE FROM KATEY

I've been A Course in Miracles student (ACIM) for over five years, and in November 2018 attended a weekend with the inspirational teachers, Hollie and Robert Holden.

It was during this magical retreat that I learnt to ask Love/God/The Divine for guidance when writing. After a short meditation to connect, the poem 'The Holy Relationship' came through me. After sharing my words and moving some of the group to tears, I decided to be more active with my communication with 'Them Lot' (as I affectionately call my spiritual team) in order to complete my bucket list wish of writing a book.

I've been writing blogs and poetry since 2014, often being woken early in the morning to be persuaded to write, but it was quite rare and felt very passive. I decided to use the same exercise from Findhorn to inspire further writing and after asking, 'Love - what would you have me know?' one night before bed, I was woken at 4 am to write. And write. And write.

This continued for an entire week and eventually I had over 50 pieces which I am delighted to share with you in this book 'What Love Told Me.'

This book is split into three categories:

# ME

Sharing my truth in all its messy glory.

# YOU

Words inspired by Holy encounters with other people.

# THEM

My Holy relationship with God/Love/Them Lot!

I encourage you to use the guidance prayer from ACIM on a daily basis to move you through your week by also asking Love:

'What would you have me do?

Where would you have me go?

What would you have me say?

And to whom?'

I find that the simple ritual of asking Love, 'What would you have me know?' helps me feel more connection to the Divine and more aligned to my purpose of BEING LOVE.

I hope you will join me on this mission.

Katey x

# CONTENTS

ME

1.

# SPECIAL WOUND

When I am with you this wound resurfaces.
Not always.
Sometimes I feel so Loved around you.
So safe.

But when your silence unsettles me, I get scared.
Your Love feels temporary as I know it could be taken
away at anytime,
And I cannot relax.

My feet get itchy.
Ready for the flight.
So I run away before you do
To stay safe.

But I fall over and knock my knees every time.
And this scab just will not heal,
No matter how many times I put a plaster over it.

## 2.
# CLOSED HEART

'Hello? Is there anyone in?' I asked my heart.
Silence.
It was all locked up with chains around it.
I knocked again.
Nothing.

*'When will she be back?'* I wondered,
As I sat down on the stone wall outside to wait.

Hours passed and still no sign of life.
She was gone.
Closed down.
Shut.

I decided I would leave a note, just in case.
I scribbled the words, 'I miss you,' and pinned it to her door
So she would know she was Loved on her return.

3.
# THE POINT OF ME

Some days I feel like my entire existence is futile.
That there's simply no point to *me*.
That I'd be better off slipping out the back door.
Not wanting to make a fuss,
Just going quietly.

But then I remember why I came here.
To fulfil my Divine Purpose:
To BE LOVE.

Which is indeed the most beautiful mission
That ever was.
And I feel
lucky
to
be
alive.

## 4.
# LONELY BUSINESS

This truth telling can be a lonely business.
Feeling like the odd one out.
Being authentic.
Being honest.
Being sad.
Being raw.


Admitting my rage and feeling shame afterwards.
Yet not keeping it private,
And brushing the broken glass under the carpet
Like the others.


I want to share with the world
All of the non-shiny, non-happy, non-perfect bits.
Confessing I am a bitch.
I am shouty.
I am mean.
I punish people.
I am frustrated.
I am angry.
I am scared.
I am unhappy.
Are you like that too?

Please be like me.

Then waiting.
For someone else to put their hand up.
Feeling really un-fucking-comfortable in the absence of
that acknowledgement.
Feeling repulsed by my own vulnerability.
Being forced to sit alone in it
While others say nothing and walk past.

And trying not to hide the exposure of my dark.
*Do not delete.*
Keeping it out there for all to see
My flaws.
Craving reassurance in the mess of it all
From just one of you.
Longing for external acceptance
Which needs to come from me.
And me alone.
Yet still wondering - *am* I just like you?

Silence.
I am just like you.
I *am* just like you.
I AM just like you.

5.
# LOST

Today I lost myself.
I looked everywhere but I was nowhere to be found.
I searched all day long in every nook and cranny.
The whole day spent calling my own name.
But I found nothing.

Then just as I was about to give up
As darkness began to fall,
I looked up and there I was.
In the whole of the sunset.

6.
# WHAT I CANNOT CARRY

You think I am strong enough to hold the world in my
arms,
And the Oceans on my back
But you do not know me.
You see what you want to see.

I cannot carry you as well.
There is simply no room,
And it is not my job.

I am also weak and tired,
And would Love to be carried
By you sometimes.
Too.

## 7.
# TOGETHER

I am braver with you.
You override my doubt with excitement,
And I see possibilities in its place.

I am stronger in the middle of all your belief.
I feel seen.
Known.

Your Love makes me invincible.
Ready to move mountains
But I cannot climb alone.

No more talk of doing this life on your own.
I need all of you.
Every single one
To see me when I cannot.
To cheer me on
As I do for you.

That is self Love.

Asking for support
So that together we can climb even higher
Than we ever could on our own.


Standing on each other's shoulders
To reach the top,
Where we can hold hands
And overlook the entire universe.

8.

# ALONE IN YOUR HEAD

I am never lonely when I am alone.
Not one bit.

I have come to enjoy my own company.
Crave it, even.

Oh no, I have always believed
The worst kind of loneliness
Is in a room packed with people.
Or with Loved ones who know you best.
Or in bed with another.

When you feel
Unheard.
Unseen.
Unknown.
Like you do not exist.
With no escape from the feeling
That you do not Matter.

Stuck with those quiet thoughts.
Alone.

Amongst the presence of others.

Trapped inside your own head
You become invisible even to yourself.

That is surely the loneliest place to be.

## 9.
# I DID SOMETHING WRONG

I did something wrong.
I know this feeling well.

The blame.
The responsibility.
The sinking feeling in my belly.

I did something wrong.

Guilt.
Shame.
Frustration.
Self-doubt.
All familiar voices.

We did something wrong.

And yet what is this new one?
A quiet voice from within whispering; 'See your own innocence.'

I did nothing wrong.

I did *nothing* wrong.

This is yours, not mine.
So I will return it back to you with shaking hands,
And know the truth.

10.
# THE CURSE

I often get taken out with this empath thing,
Calling it a curse.
Wishing I was different.
Less sensitive.

'Poor me,' I complain.
'It's so difficult feeling so much.'

And God only laughs, as She sets up the film reel of my
happiest memories:

Tears of joy above a volcano,
Dancing around the Big Orange Rock at sunset,
Cycling over canals in the snow,
Or simply sitting on a sofa drinking tea and laughing.

'Oops, I forgot all that,' I say,
Feeling ungrateful as my cheeks turn pink.
Realising how hard can it be to feel so much
When you get to Love the whole world
every
single

day
in return?

And God smiles as I finally remember
What it is to be me.

11.
# WRONG AUDIENCE

Funny how in this performance of life
I ignore the ones at the front,
Cheering me on,
Singing all of the words.

I focus instead on the ones at the back,
Chatting amongst themselves
With no interest in being there.
With no idea of my name.
They don't even recognise the tune.

And yet I look to them for validation
Which of course never comes,
Begging them to buy my records in desperation.

No wonder I feel so deflated after each gig,
Trying to win over the wrong audience with my music.

12.
# CHOSEN

I want to be chosen.
To be pointed out in the crowd
As the one who would be next,
So it would finally be my turn
To be picked.

I hear myself harping on about
Feeling second best,
As if there's a competition
Where I always get silver or bronze.

Always pipped to the post
By the ones on the highest block
Wearing the gold.

I envy them.
Comparison hiding my true self.
Feeling shame towards my inferiority
For all to see,
Judging my weakness.

Even though it is my own fault.
My own laziness.

Since I have never once stood up there on those blocks,
Declaring to the world in an unshakeable voice
That I was ready.

To actually choose myself

And pick me.

13.
# THE APOLOGY

You talk of toxic masculinity,
Of the patriarchy,
Like it is something outside of us.

All one-sided.
All their fault.
And that we are the only innocent party.

But I'm sorry, Sisters;
I want to own up as I feel too guilty for my side.
Since deep down I know we are both to blame.

This longing to confess
That despite how they have treated us,
I don't feel good about the way I treated them either.

I have deemed them as spineless,
Shallow,
Pathetic,
Weak.

I have fuelled the divide by lumping them all together
with a dismissive, 'They're all the same.'

I have been the abuser,
The bully,
The manipulator.

The equivalent of a 'misogynist,' if you will.
Although I doubt there is an actual word invented for us.

But all this men bashing
Only contributes to the 'Them and Us' separation.

And I want us to join together.
To forgive the past.

So I will not speak for any of you,
But if you disagree, dear sisters,
Then remember,
This is MY truth, not yours.
Although I'm sure you will have your own version.
Your own guilt.

We all do.

So here is my part.
My humble apology.
To the men who have crossed my path.

I apologise to my brothers
For thinking you were all the same.
For continuing the belief that, 'You can't rely on a man, so
I might as well do it myself,'
From generations that weren't even mine.

For trying to match you pint for pint,
Talking about shagging,
Swearing,
The banter,
Taking the piss,
Trying to fit in with some of you and pretending that was
fun for me.

For showing you the tough exterior
And hiding my emotions.
For lying about who I am.

For hating the porn industry
But still acting like the porn star,
And pretending that was ok.

For the blame I carried towards YOU
From MY ancestors,
Towards your ancestors,
Not YOU.


For bitching about you to the collective sisterhood
And contributing to the separation.


For thinking we were superior
Because we cope with periods and have babies
And don't get 'Man Flu.'


For the time I dismissed your offer of help
With a derogatory 'I'm fine,'
When I struggled with my suitcase
Down the steps to The Tube.
Then took great significance that I could do it myself.
That I was just as strong as you.


For always taking the bin out myself
And getting pissed off that
'I have to do everything around here,'


For making you doubt whether to open a door for me
Because you'd been barked at,
Or beaten to it with an 'I got it' so many times.

For expecting you to be a mind reader
And punishing you when you weren't
Because I hadn't learned how to state my needs.

For not communicating properly.
For answering 'Fine,' then kicking into Ice Queen mode,
And giving you the silent treatment.

For rolling my eyes when you couldn't do something And
saying, 'For God's sake - I'll do it,'
Rather than encouraging and empowering you.

For nagging and trying to get you to
Change who you are.

For Mothering you.
For Smothering you.

For not looking up to you
Or acknowledging the things you do for me.

For all the times I judged you for letting me down,
When I let myself down.

I especially cringe about the times
When I wouldn't back down when you *did* show up.

When I didn't trust your glorious masculine.
When you did dare to show it,
I belittled it,
I laughed it off,
I refused to surrender.
I met yours with mine and I tried to out-do you.
Two masculines at loggerheads with each other

And remember -
I was carrying the generational
Warrior Women on my back
Who had to fight so hard,
Who *were* left alone to do everything.
So of course you didn't stand a chance.

You were always going to lose and give in first. 'Anything
for a quiet life.'
Back down.
And leave me smug that I'd won.

But you failed the test.
And I am deeply sorry that I set the trap for you.
You backing down meant I got to continue
The story that *all* men are untrustworthy.
'See? I have to be the Man *and* the woman
In this relationship.'

So finally, and this is the hardest one to say -
For all the times I screamed at you to 'Man up,'
When I couldn't 'man down' myself.
I didn't know how to.
I was never taught.
But I know now and I promise to do that
As often as I can catch myself.
And when you remind me.


And for everything else that has passed between us Where
you have felt less-than,
Punished,
Hurt,
Confused,
Disrespected,
I am deeply sorry.
I chose significance over Love so I wouldn't get hurt.
Again.
Protecting myself.
Not letting you in.
Allowing you into my body but never my heart.


But my core is feminine and yours is masculine.
I want to relax into that feminine as much as possible.
Now.
I am tired of being masculine around you.
And herein lies the confusion.

The contradiction.
The huge grey areas.

I need my masculine to get stuff done,
To face challenges,
To do my work.

I need my feminine to be in flow,
To be creative,
To trust,
To receive.

As you do,
As we have both parts within us.

So you see?
We *are* the same yet totally different.
But I commit to somehow celebrating our differences as
Beautiful,
Sacred,
Mysterious,
Rather than as something to punish each other for
And to further fuel the great divide
Which only brings hurt,
Pain,
And more separation.

I want Connection and Oneness.
As you do.


So we have to hold hands and do it together.


To use our polarity to return to our core.


 I want my Divine Feminine to continue emerging
And at the same time empower your confidence
That you are safe to return to your Divine Masculine.


Thank you for everything you are.
I see you.
I Love you.
I'm sorry I hurt you too.

# YOU

14.
# THE MOTHER

'You'll leave me like they all do,' he said.
I took it as a challenge to prove that out of all of
Womankind there was one who could Love him.

So I put up my Batfink wings and took you under them.
Trying to protect you,
Trying to Love you
Like she should have.

I judged her as being a terrible mother -
How could she give you away like that?

The ultimate betrayal by the one whose only job
Was to Love you.

And because she didn't,
I knew that it was up to me
Since I found Love so easy.

But you tested me too many times
And my heart got tired of trying to prove itself.

And it was never my job actually.

So I also had to let you go in the end,
Just like she had when you were born.

When I gave in you seemed relieved
That you could go on,
Continuing to feel unlovable.

And believing your own story.

## 15.
# FIRST KISS

There was so much riding on that first kiss.
It almost happened so many times.
Unable to make eye contact,
We shyly looked down at our feet.
And yet we both still wondered if our lips could sing
together.

By the water that day,
With butterflies flitting in my stomach,
I thought you had changed your mind,
That I must have been mistaken.

But in no time at all you were ready,
Racing towards me,
So full of courage and not thinking this time.

Ready to test these feelings.
'It's time, darling.'
Both of us quietly terrified,
As our lips finally joined together.

'Nobody saw that coming,' you joked,
Relieved.

And you kissed me again.

And every day since.

16.
# THE BLAME

I could be angry at you,
Neglecting my precious body,
Shutting my heart down.

The rejection made me mad with shame.
The hot rage came through me,
And all of my frustration crashed out wildly.

It scared you.

But my body was confused.
It longed to be Loved.
To be touched.
But you could not.
Would not.

There is no anger now,
Only sadness.
And regret at the blame I threw at you
In all my pain.
When yours was so much bigger.

But it wasn't your fault, my Love,
And I am so deeply sorry
For all that was.
For all that *never* was.
For it all.

And now I am free.
I often wonder if you are too.

17.
# THE DEVIL AND THE ANGEL

You rage at me,
Screaming that you are The Devil
And I am The Angel,
Always showing you up
With my goodness.

Oh no, you're wrong.
My heart is just as dark as yours.
And that light you see is only your own,
Reflected in my eyes.

18.
# SHINE ON, BELOVED

Look at you over there,
Shining like a beacon for all to see.
Your light is radiant.
Infectious.
It lights up the room
And illuminates everyone in it.

Look at you now,
Laughing merrily at your own reflection.
Meeting your eyes with wonder
As you choose to see joy these days.

You sparkle like you have never known darkness,
Relieved to have left it behind.
No longer scared of it showing up again
As you know how to confront it now.

Blasting from your heart
It would be startled by your full beam.
Shielding its eyes,
Fearful of all the Love you have inside you now,
The Love that is here to stay.

Amongst all of it -
The light and the dark.

Shine on beloved one.
This is your time.

Shine on.

19.
# STAYING

'Can we be enough?' he asked me gruffly,
Attempting to hide the vulnerability through his tone.
'I don't know,' I answered truthfully. 'Surely there needs
to be more?'

I winced.

'Not for me.'

But here it was again; this feeling of not knowing.
The indecision.

Doubting myself,
Not him.

'I cannot trust myself to know,' I tried to explain.
'I've always got it so wrong before.'

Being passive,

Searching for clues and signs that distracted me,
And took me far away from what I actually wanted.

'What do YOU want?'

Why was that question so big for me?

He was silently asking it of me now.
Of the future.

I answered in the present.
'All I know is that today, I choose you, and you choose
me.'

'And what will you say tomorrow?' he asked.

'I don't know, my Love,
But I promise that every single day
I will ask my heart the questions
Of what it needs,
And what its truth is.
And whatever it replies,
I shall do that.'

I see the pain on his face at the uncertainty of it all.
Of what's to come.

So I ask him, 'Can that be enough?'
And of course he also does not know.

20.
# THE HOLY RELATIONSHIP

You questioned me about this other man.
This person more 'suitable'.
More compatible.

'Go be with him,' you said.
'Leave. Go to him.'

He who I Loved more than you.

'There is no one else,' I told you.
'No one but you.'

I lied.
You were right all along.
There was someone else
But I couldn't admit the truth,
And I didn't want to introduce you.

The time, the circumstance, the moment
For you to finally meet this other man wasn't up to me.
You had to meet him first yourself

So that you could laugh and say, 'Hello old friend,'
And realise your rival was never that.
Not your competition at all,
But a dear friend
Whom you would recognise and declare,
'So you're the one who distracted her,
That shared her heart
And showed her how to Love.'


And you would remember Him
Since you've met him before,
So often.
In me.


The many times you glimpsed Him in my smile.
In the way I laugh.
In my eyes.


You were right about His presence;
There was always another in this relationship.


But you looked in the wrong places for his existence.
Forgetting to look in the most obvious place.
Inside your heart.


But you needed to meet Him first alone.
In you.

46

Meet Him in your self.
So that the three of us could all hold hands and laugh
As we declared our Love together.

And now you and He will share my Love,
After all what's mine is yours.
And His.

And because this Holy third,
Who was in you all along,
Has the capacity to Love us both,
Even when we are unable to.

So you must trust me now you know the truth.
Now you understand why I chose Him over you.
His is the Love we have both been seeking.

So let it in

Let Him Love us both,
And show us the truth of our union.
This trio of Holiness
In the three of us.

Together.

21.
# BONES

'Go on,' she said, 'don't you want to know what it feels
like to be me?'
She'd got me.
I was intrigued.

The chance to experience being someone else
Was too tempting.
To imagine not being me for a moment.

I jumped right in and she seemed happy
That I wanted to understand her.

But all I saw was sadness.
Heightened in this state.
The emptiness made worse in the morning.

I was cold in my bones, being her.
I shivered and could not get warm.
My mouth tasted rancid.
I felt like a shadow.

Why would she choose this?
How could this possibly help her to exist?

I still didn't get it.

I had glimpsed what it was to be her
And I didn't like it one bit.

But at least for one moment she had felt
Known.
And seen.
And understood.
In the loneliness of everything she was.

And that made it all worth it.

22.
# SHADOW

'It's bad, darling.'
The phone call from across the water
Seemed like a dream.
Or a nightmare, rather.


Your voice never faltered as you told me everything.
I listened in disbelief at the story of death
And destruction.
You were calm - reporting to me like it was a tragedy
You'd seen on the news.
Happening to someone else.
But it was all yours.


He'd taken them both with him to their death.
Him.
Her.
Almost you.


But you refused.


I never knew you were so strong.
Imagine little you standing up to him

Who towered above you.
So tough.

I felt like I didn't know you for a moment -
My 'little Dutch sister' who I always looked after,
Making you English tea and running around for,
As you lazed on the sofa.

And now this -
So unafraid,
So fierce,
You fought him for your life.

Motherhood must have made you into a lioness,
With a roar so mighty that somehow,
Through a miracle of your sheer force,
You were still here.
You got out.
Against the odds.

I cried silent tears down the phone.
You got out.
Thank Christ you got out.

I felt shame for feeling relief,
When your baby boy was gone.

To try to assuage my own guilt,
I pointlessly bartered with the truth.
Why could it not have been both of them
Who managed to struggle free?
Could they not have both lived?
Why couldn't he have just left him behind?
How could a father harm his own child?
I was livid.


The anger began to bubble
But I kept it away from my tone
As you were so peaceful.
Serene almost.
The shock perhaps?
But no, something more.
Presence.
To it all.
You sounded like an angel.


And clearly he had been the devil.


As the call ended,
I felt my own force of evil come through.
This was new to me.
Shocked by the strength of it, I *needed* to run.
*From* it?

*To* it?
*Fuelled* by it?


As I pulled on my running shoes I could see his face.
I could feel the red mist descending,
Blood pulsing through my veins.
Pure hatred.
So I ran and ran.
As if I was chasing him, spurred on the repulsion I felt. My
feet moving faster than ever.
Hatred consuming me.
White rage towards him.
I also wanted to kill.
Like he had.


The noise of my own darkness purged out of me
And stopped me in my tracks.
I had never seen these emotions up close.
My feeble heart had avoided them so far,
But here I was being forced into feeling them all,
Like it or not.


Anger.
Rage.
Sadness.
Confusion.
Injustice.

Fear.
My shadow side here at last.
The real work had begun.


And I cried like a wounded animal -
For it all.
For you,
For your son,
And for her.


But not for him.


No way.
I spat out my disgust and more tears came
When I realised that I was just like him.
That I too possessed that violence,
If only in thoughts.
And so I cried for my guilty angry heart
Who could only choose pain and hate.
Like he had.


And after what seemed like only hours later,
My plane was landing,
And I was in the same country as you again.
Where everyone knew the story.
Where you were all over the news and in the papers. And I
felt satisfied that more people would hate him too. That a

54

whole nation would be judging him
And what he had done.
Just like I did.


I was still raging as I got out of the taxi at the crematorium,
trying to keep my angry tears at bay, until I walked into
that room and saw you.


My heart exploded.
A few precious moments observing you, unnoticed.
You seemed so grown up.
So comfortable in your skin.
How can this be?
You radiated joy and happiness while others openly cried.


I had half expected the shock to have worn off, that you
would be sat in the corner sobbing and being the grieving
mother in black.


But no, this was the opposite - you seemed to be this
powerhouse of strength and I felt ashamed towards myself
for having been in the drama and the pain, when you
seemed to have chosen only grace and Love.
In fact, you weren't just choosing Love - you *were* Love.
Love that now knew no fear.
The worst had already happened.

When our eyes finally connected, I realised that even
though you had lost so much, you had never looked so
completely whole.

Even with all that death you had never looked so alive.
And despite all that pain; you had never possessed such
beauty.  And such light.

You walked towards me, smiling, despite this painful
reunion and I felt only awe that even in the middle of all
this darkness, your tender broken heart was filled with a
light that seemed to be the size of the entire fucking
Universe.

And you continued to beam your light in the days, months
and now years on. And I could not be more proud, my
darling, brave, incredible friend.

Thank you.

23.
# L O S S

I see her sitting quietly on her bench softly crying.
She seems oblivious to the tears mixing with the rain water
on her face.
It's dark.

I approach her.
'I see you,' I say silently,
But the inevitable 'Are you okay?' is what actually comes
out.

'Of course not,' her eyes reply,
But the lie 'I'm fine,' is spoken.

Neither of us believes her.

'May I sit?' I speak, with the rest of the words
Hanging in the air. 'May I quietly witness your pain?
Will you show me your truth?'

Her heart, raw and open responds.
'I will show you. It is too much for me to carry alone
tonight.'

She sips on her bottle.
Archers.
The sickly sweet smell transports me back in time for a
moment,
And I lose my presence.
She offers me a cigarette then when I refuse,
Apologises for the smoke.


'How did you see me?'
She seems surprised.


I tell her I see a lot of people sitting on this bench.
In their grief.
Remembering.


'I come here to be with her.'
'Do you talk to her?' I ask.
'All the time.'
'What does she say?'
'Many things. Usually she asks me to come and join her,
But I haven't managed it yet.'


The 'yet' hangs between us.


She talks about her loss of her beautiful girl,
In the prime of her life.
She talks about death.

How she plans her own daily.
How her brain has decided that she must also stop Being.
How every time she has tried,
She gets saved
At the last minute.

To me it is a great wonder the pills remain untouched in
her pocket.

Given the choice between this life without her
and death, I am bewildered why she would choose to stay.

'What stops you?' I want to ask. 'Why would you, when
she's calling you so loudly from the other side?'

But I do not dare in case my asking sparks her into action.
Nudges her over.
And for a moment I panic.
I move into fixer.
Helper.
How can I stop her?
How can I save her?
I've been put on her path tonight.
But what the hell can I do?
Show me.
Show me.
Show me.

Luckily she's tired.
It won't be tonight.
We both know.
I feel relieved.
She feels weak.
Maybe tomorrow.


She stands up to leave and I ask if she needs a hug.
As I embrace her, I hold on a little longer.
Perhaps for myself rather than her.
As I'll never know whether she'll make it.

24.
# HOLY KITTEN

I swear this kitten is God.

He can transform my tired heart with just one glance;
Winking both eyes,
Meowing, 'Good Morning,'
And delivering me back to Love.

Which makes me think that surely he *is* the Holy instant In cat disguise.

25.

# OLD TREE

I find myself again stood at the roots of this old tree.
There are so many Great Oaks in these woods,
Yet I spend my time with this rotten one.

Hoping my encouragement will somehow coax it to grow
new leaves and reverse the dying process.

But even though its branches are bare and rotting,
It continues to selfishly feed on the earth
With no interest in the rest of the forest.

Refusing to acknowledge the unfulfilled potential of that
tiny acorn from years ago

I wonder why I spend my time here watching it begin its
slow death
Rather than being amongst the others,
Who already whisper my name on the wind.

This is not my tree, I realise.

I walk away for the last time,
Brushing its trunk lovingly with my fingers.

And I go off in search of another to carve my initials into instead.

26.

# ANOTHER LIFETIME

'Remember me?' you asked excitedly,
Waiting for a spark of recognition.
I always had a terrible memory.
'It's me! From way back!'

I looked deeply into your eyes.
They must be the same, I thought,
Staring more deeply.
Still confused.

But my heart answered first.
'Of Course! It's YOU! You're back!'
We embraced,
Feeling the Love return in a split second
Before I remembered.

And pulled away.

'This is not our time, my Love' I said sadly.

'What are you talking about, dear beloved?'
You were incredulous. 'This is it! Our big reunion after all
this time.'

In your bones I think you also knew,
You just didn't want to admit it
After all this time apart.

I also hoped and tried to figure out a way,
But it was not to be.

If we had Love's blessing,
All the doors would open.
All the lights would change to green.
And the path ahead would be clear.

But alas there were simply too many blocks.
Too many obstacles.

I knew you were no longer mine,
In this lifetime at least.
We had our chances back then.
Over and over.

I could see tears in your eyes
As I was already preparing to let you go.

Quietly knowing
That we would meet again.
For the thousandth time
In another version of us.

Next time.

27.
# KING

I spent all that time searching for the handsome Prince.
Kissing a lot of frogs,
And waiting in vain for their transformation.
Trying to convince spineless knaves
To scale the castle walls.

Trying to mould them and shape them into Royalty.
Wondering if one would *ever* turn up on his white horse.

But still I remained locked in the tower.
Waiting.
Waiting.
Waiting.

Doubting that I would ever be the fairest of them all for
someone.

Then one fine day you arrived in the Kingdom.
Not on a horse, but a dragon.
Ready to slay anything that would get in your way.

Prepared to fight and chop down my walls with your
sword

You were nothing like the others.
I had never met anyone as brave.
Or fierce.
Or strong.

Perhaps because you were never a Prince.
Or a knight.

You asked to see the Queen, and when I told you,
'There is only me here, a lonely Princess in this castle,'
You refused to believe it,
And barricaded yourself into my heart.

Waiting patiently

Until the fearful Princess melted away
And I finally stepped up,
In all my sovereignty,
To meet my King.

Ready to choose the happily ever after
Demanding it.

As Queens do.
For both of us.

28.
# SEARCH FOR LOVE

'How's your search for love going?' he asked, only weeks
after we had met.
'Pretty badly,' I replied, and promptly burst into tears.

But that was the opening,
And my heart Loved him immediately.
Knowing we had work to do together.
That familiarity.
That Recognition.
Hinting at a future.

Like the psychic had,
When she told me I would be packing boxes
And moving across water.
That future which was not to be.

She had got some parts right.
I *had* crossed the water;
Exactly one year after that serendipitous meeting
Where he'd recognised me
From his window above the canal,

Only 24-hours after sitting in the seat next to me,
The previous day.


Both of us unaware that this chance encounter,
With 'That Dutch guy from the plane'
Shouting my name from across the water,
Would later change the course of our lives forever.


But True 'Love' never did run smoothly.
And the cards had lied about the other things.
The wedding.
The baby.
The happiness.


I probably would have left sooner if they *had* told the truth.


So I stayed.
For an entire decade.
Still hoping.
Still trying.
Still avoiding the truth.


Feeling all of the pain.
The tears.
The rejection.
The loneliness.
Yours and mine.

71

Both of us addicted to feeling worthless.
Playing out our shadow.
Convinced it was Love.

And I wonder now who I would be
Had it never happened.
Surely it was just coincidence that of all the 165 canals,
I happened to cycle along his.

But no, there was no way we could have not met
Since Love had organised it all.
To learn the lesson.
To get the healing.
To stay for as long as I did so that I could lose myself
So completely.

That my heart would remember in the nick of time
To direct my search towards me instead,
Rather than him,
And set me back on the Path to Love.

True Love.
For my Self.

29.
# UNHAPPY
# CURRICULUM

The two of us held hands, skipping home from school.

'What did you do today?' I asked.
'We learnt the key to happiness,' he replied.
'Wow, that's big,' I said, amused. 'So tell me what you learnt.'

'Whenever you don't feel happy, all you have to do is squeeze your thumb and your finger together really tight like this then you feel happy again.  And you don't have to feel any of the bad feelings ever again.'

'Erm, what kind of 'bad' feelings?'

'Y'know, like sad or angry or frustrated, those kind of things.'

I stopped in the middle of the pavement, horrified.
And crouched down, still holding his hand.
I tried to keep my voice calm.

'I am stopping to tell you something very important.'

His big, beautiful eyes looked up expectantly at my imminent lecture.

'What they taught you today darling is complete nonsense.

Sometimes in life things will happen and you will feel all of those things but you do not need to push them away. Or change how you feel or try to get happy again.

Some days you WILL just feel sad or scared or unhappy and no matter what anyone tells you, it is ok to feel those things.'

'But Miss told me it's better to turn a frown upside down.'

I winced and took a sharp inhale of breath.

'No darling. You don't ever have to be happy for other people. Just feel whatever you feel even if it's uncomfortable. All of your feelings are ok.

And nothing you do or feel will make us Love you any less.

Whether you're happy or sad or excited or angry.

We will always Love you. In all of it.'

*Good speech*, I congratulated myself.
*Now I just have to remember it for myself.*

30.
# TRIBE

To the ones: My Ones.
Who are there every single time my tender heart steps out
onto the tightrope.
High above,
Terrified with wobbling knees.

The ones who cheer from down below,
'You can do this,' as they smile up at me reassuringly.

Each holding a corner of the safety net,
Ready to catch me if I fall.

Which of course I don't,
Since their belief holds me steady.

To those ones,
I give gratitude.

My heart always feels safe in your hands.

Thank you for being there for me in this ongoing circus.

31.

# BEAUTIFUL GRIEF

My dear friend – I see you sat alone in your sadness
With grief seeping out of every pore.
Layers and layers of emotion.
Too much to feel.

I want to give you a huge chunk of time
So that tomorrow you could wake in the future
With a healed heart.

But your pain is beautiful,
Important even.

Because it shows the world that you know how to Love.

32.
# BLOCKS TO LOVE

'Your capacity to be loved,' she told him, 'is in direct correlation with how unremarkable you think you are.'

'Wow that much?' he replied, bored.

She paused for a moment, before proceeding to point out all of the flaws in the rest of his plans to block Love.

He raised an eyebrow at her smugness,
Ending the conversation with a smirk.

## 33.
# HEART CAFE

There you go again,
With your big heart pouring out of your shirt sleeves.
Sneaking small droplets into someone else's soup.

You put your coat on and tiny crystals of light are flung
around the room,
Landing in the sugar bowls on the tables.

As you go to leave, you secretly scatter a shining trail of
heart-shaped diamonds behind you.
To light the way for those who are hungry or lost.

That mammoth heart of yours could easily feed
Every single person on the planet.
And still have enough leftovers for second helpings.

34.
# BELONGING

Thank you for carrying me
When I was tired and ready to give in.
Thank you for showing me my truth
When all I heard was lies from my own lips.
Thank you for seeing me
When I was invisible to most.
Thank you for believing in me
When my own doubt was so loud.
Thank you for knowing me
When I was a stranger to my own heart.
And for showing I mattered
When I didn't matter to myself.
Thank you for showing me my own beauty
Just simply by being so beautiful yourself.
My dear mirror.
My soul twin.
My other half.
Thank you.
Your heart will always have a home in mine.
And you will always belong in the world.

35.

# THE STORM

I do not want to fight anymore.
The storm outside is loud enough,
Raging away on its own.
Like we do.

Trying to be heard over this thunder inside.
The wind howls in harmony with us.
The rain bangs on the window
But there's so much noise we do not notice.

The trees are worried,
As are we in our hearts,
Longing for it to pass.

I do not want to be the enemy any more.
Love cannot win this time.
When we fight of the same things,
Going round in circles.
Insisting that we both want peace
Yet repeating the same cruel things.

Over and over.
Fighting our own corner.
Never listening.
Both lost in battles with ourselves.
As well as each other.

Can we not rest awhile,
And warm our cold hearts by this fire?
The storm will continue without us anyway.
This weather makes me tired.

Let us lie down and sleep
And leave our hearts to talk together in peace,
And return us back to Love
In the Morning
Instead.

36.
# TEACHER

This kitten teaches me about love every day.
How unconditional it should be,
And how we humans get it so wrong
Trying to change and fix each other.

I do not expect him to be something he's not.
Not wishing he was a dog or a fish or a bird.
Not telling him, 'Well you're very cute but it's a shame
you can't fly.'
Or asking him to bark and fetch a stick.

Nor do I try to change his fur into beautiful orange scales
And throw him into the pond to force him to swim.

I am not angry with him when he stays out all night,
Playing with other cats.
And when he sleeps all day,
I don't judge him as lazy.

If he is aloof I do not punish him,
Instead give him the space he needs.
And when he is needy,

Demanding cuddles by sitting on my chest,
I give him my full attention.

I accept his Kitten-ness,
Exactly as he is.
That's just what kittens do.

And I Love him completely
Without any expectations that he will evolve
To become something other than a cat.

I hope I come back as a cat in my next life.
It seems so much more simple
Than being a human.

## 37.
# THE BUBBLE

We are safe in here.
Happy even.
No one can touch us.
Our love is so fulfilling
And whole.

I want to stay forever in this space
With it enveloping us,
Protecting us from the outside.
Just me and you,
No one else.

Can it be enough?
The unspoken question
With such an obvious answer.

Of course not.

I want more.
I need more.
But we carry on pretending in our cosy bubble
Until inevitably it bursts.

Each time the world sucks us back in
Leaving us alone with our opposing fears.

The engulfment.
The abandonment.
And yet united by the separation.

38.

# THE AMERICAN

You clocked me straight away,
Saw through my lies
And called out the game show host,
Inviting her up on stage.

'It's time,' you said, as you cheered and demanded high
fives
In the American way as I rolled my eyes, laughing.

I felt smug as you talked about my energy lighting up
rooms.
How others saw me.
Funny.
Happy.
Loving.

I sat quietly smiling into the audience with significance.
My confidence didn't last,
As you called bullshit and waded straight in.
Out of the blue, in front of all these people,
Exposing the hidden truth of my sadness.

My shame.
My grief.


And the exhaustion of pretending,
Acknowledging it all for the first time.


I wondered how you had known.
How I was so transparent to you.


I was stunned, yet the tears flowed with relief to be finally
seen.
But then my stomach sank as you welcomed my anger to
the stage.


'What anger?' I acted innocently.
Still the denial.
But it had been my secret.
And mine alone.


Not anymore.
Too late -
You'd seen it all.


'Ready to give this anger a voice?' you asked,
Handing over the microphone and asking to hear it.

I recoiled in horror.
'Oh God, no,' I pleaded.
But he stepped back and I was centre stage
In front of my American sisters,
With tears in their eyes.

Silently loving me.
Willing me on.

I stood there shaking.
Doubting myself.
Afraid to be heard.

And then out of nowhere
The tiniest sound like a dying animal
Whimpering,
From this hidden place within,
Yet getting louder and louder.

My tender heart beginning to wail.
Even louder now.
Coming up from inside of my bones.

And then finally this noise
That surely could not belong to me,

This almighty roar
Thundering out of my own heart.


The rage.


The raw, honest, rage.
Screaming out of me.
Coming out of the shadows.
'ENOUGH,' it shouted.
And then nothing.


Silence.


Empty with relief that it had gone,
And yet something new its place now.


Everyone held their breath as it rushed in,
Filling the space with this brightness.
With love and connection.
What the hell....?


The light has come.
The light has come.
The light has come.

And I smiled.

Laughter now amongst the tears.

And you held me and whispered, 'I see you,

As I cried with the joy

Of facing a darkness that I'd kept so well hidden


From everyone but you.

39.

# LONE TRAVELLER

I ran away from home
So many times,
Packing everything into one backpack
And doing a runner to travel the world.
Trying to get as far away as possible
From Myself, probably.

Seeking solace in the four corners of the globe.
Getting so good at saying goodbye.
Out of sight out of mind.
Managing to breathe on the most fleeting of connections,
Safe in the intimacy, born from knowing
Our paths would never cross again.

Living amongst strangers.
Choosing to be the Foreigner,
The outsider,
The tourist,
The backpacker.

Always Me, myself and I.

Ignoring my hearts impatience
To take a risk on actual belonging.

I am happiest alone, I kidded myself.
But what a cunning tactic to keep my heart protected
All that time,
Always moving on.
Packing up each time things got too close.
Hiding from the very thing I longed for.

So imagine my surprise, when my heart,
Tired of all the empty connection
And longing to sleep in its own bed,
Booked me on the first flight back to the very place I
started.

Having known all along
That home was always something inside of me.

# THEM

40.
# THE EARLY HOURS

Love woke me in the early hours.
I protested, wanting to sleep.
But She kept shaking me to wake up.

'Go away,' I pleaded, 'it's the middle of the night.'
But She turned the light on and shone it right in my face.

'How can you sleep when there is so much beauty in the darkness?'
And she thrust me a pen and paper.
'Love cannot write itself,' she told me.

And I gave in and began to scribble as she dictated the words:

'Even in the dark I am there knowing the truth of your very existence.'

41.
# LOVE WARRIOR

To be loved in such a way where there is no doubt or fear
Is surely one of the most wondrous feelings there is.


To be seen without flaws or ugliness by another
Is so reassuring to our own tired eyes
That we are forced to look again
To see what they see,
Asking curiously, 'How on earth could you Love this?'


To be Loved in wholeness brings such strength and
courage.
Power.
Faith.
Connection.


When those eyes are on us,
Staring lovingly at ALL of it
The way you do.


We can see ourselves differently,
And we look ten feet tall

Like warriors,
Capable of winning any battle.

42.
# TRUST

Go on, trust Love
Just one more time.

You've been hurt before
And you got out alive.

So try again.
In fact don't try,
Just do.
Or rather be.

Let's face it,
It will end badly
Either way.

In Death or worse.
Choosing another over you.

But you can do it.
You've done it a million times.
It is so easy to you.

It is in your blood.
In that great heart of yours.

So go on.
Deep breath.
Jump back in.
It is time.

Love is waiting
To catch you.

Again.

43.
# LOVE'S BEDROOM

'Wakey wakey, lazy bones.'
A rude awakening.

I open my eyes to the morning light, wondering whose voice it is today.

It's Fear.

'Good morning, rise and shine,' he says as he draws back the curtains.

'Oh it's you,' I say wearily.

'I'm here too,' said the quiet shy voice of Love, but Fear talks over her, as usual.

'C'mon, get up - we have so much to do.' He drags the covers off me.

Love just rolls her eyes as she pulls the duvet back over herself.

I step out of bed and Fear trips me up.

'Ha ha gotcha!'

I am tearful,
Wobbly,
Raw.
I look longingly at Love but she's fallen back to sleep.

Fear drags me to the bathroom,
And as I look in the mirror,
He snidely tells me how rough I look.

I stare at my reflection,
Searching for Love's best friend Kindness,
But only the Evil twins rock up -
Bossiness and Meanness.

'Good morning,' they chirp simultaneously.

'Why are you two so perky?' I ask, but they're too busy
inspecting my frizzy hair and sniggering.

'Ok we have a busy day ahead of us, let's get a move on
shall we,' says Bossiness as he orders me into the shower,
while Meanness gives my naked body the once over and

makes some comment to the others out of earshot.
I pull the shower curtain around me but can still hear them
whispering about me.

I wash and dry myself quickly. My energy is flat but they
usher me into the bedroom to get dressed. My clothes feel
too big and I wonder if I have shrunk in the night.

'Wow, you're very small today,' said Fear.

'Look at the state of you,' quips Meanness, 'you can't go
out looking like that.'

'We haven't got time for all this messing,' says Bossiness,
'we have to get things done, remember.'

We go downstairs and there is Significance looking at his
watch. 'What time do you call this? We are so busy. Let's
Go Go Go. Chop Chop.'

'What's the plan of attack?' asks Fear.

'Well, clearly this loser is incapable of organising things
today so we'll have to do everything for her,' says
Meanness, 'we need a meeting.' And they huddle together,
each of them shouting over the other.

No one notices as I sneak out and go back upstairs.

Love is awake. She's sitting in bed reading and drinking tea.

'I'm tired,' I tell her, 'I can't do it today. It's all too much.'

She draws back the covers and beckons me in. 'Well, get back in here with us, my dear,' and I notice Kindness in there too. These two are inseparable after all. I get in and Kindness speaks softly: 'That bunch of fools will be fine without you today,' as she starts stroking my hair and my face.

'Don't worry, we'll look after you today,' says Love. 'You need some nurturing. Some rest,' and I start to relax as she cuddles me.

She looks in my tired, tearful eyes and whispers, 'Darling girl, there is nothing you need to do or be today. You are enough without the busyness. And sometimes you just can't do it, and that's ok. Now rest your weary heart, my dear, and start again tomorrow. We'll stay with you,' and Kindness nods with her.

And I sigh as I fall back to sleep in Love's arms, feeling her rocking me gently, whispering my name.

## 44.
# LOVING IT ALL

I am suspicious of Love.
I do not trust Her flowery words and compliments.
When she says, 'I Love you,'
I narrow my eyes,
Waiting for a 'but..'
Or a special clause to highlight a circumstance or
behaviour where conditions may apply.

'Ok Love, can you Love my ugliness when I judge others
to make myself feel better?'

'Yes dear.'

'Hmm, well what about when I'm nasty and bitchy about
people because I feel worthless inside?'

'Yes of course.'

'Right. And what about when I'm punishing and dishing
out emotional invoices when I'm hurt, or I resent those I
Love? Or when I feel rejected?' I say, trying to trip her up.

She doesn't take the bait.

'Yes, all of that as well.'

'Can you Love my anger when I feel stupid or confused?
In the middle of injustice when I want to attack back ?
Or in my shame which I throw out as rage?'

Love rolls her eyes, nodding.

'I see through all of those things, dear heart.'

I rack my brains, hoping to catch her out.
Scanning all of my darkness for something definitely
unlovable.

I speak again but it comes out as a whisper.
'Can you Love me when I feel small and full of doubt.
Or when the pain is too much and the sadness unbearable,
so much so that I want to disappear from the world? When
I just don't know how to be me anymore, And I no longer
want to exist?'

A tear rolls down my face as I admit my worst truth.

Love knows.

'Especially then. I will always be there for you on those days too. When you cannot Love yourself. Or me. But I will still throw my arms around you and kiss your face over and over until you smile and remember the beauty of your own heart. And I will continue to Love you. All of you. Because you *are* as much Love as I am. And you are so easy to Love.

Since Love is Love is Love is Love is Love.'

45.
# LOVE'S HOME

Whenever you think you fail at Love,
Time and time again,
Love is still there, regardless.

Loving you in all your doubt and fear,
Waiting patiently,
To remind your separate lonely heart
Of your own Innocence
And bring you Home.

46.
# THE SACRED MEETING

'What is this Holy encounter?' I asked God one day.

'It is the chatty lady in the queue you let in front of you.

It is the apology from the shop assistant who was a bit brusque.

It is the hidden smirk from an eavesdropper to your daft conversations on the bus.

It is in your friend's tears as she shares her heartbreak with you.

It is when for a split second you lock eyes with a stranger and you recognise my face in theirs.
And you both smile as you remember that
EVERYONE was made from Love.

That is this Holiness I speak of.'

47.
# THE ORDER OF MIRACLES

I never think to ask for a miracle.
Surely they are only reserved for other people
In big grown up situations
With serious problems.

But apparently Love has no favourites
When it comes to dishing out the good stuff,
And that anytime we feel taken down by life,
All we need to do is ask.

That's all.
It's that easy.

And once Love's HQ receives the request,
They will manage all the admin and paperwork. Crossing
the t's and dotting the i's.

Sometimes they even send God Herself downstairs
To reassure us that our order is being processed,
And all we need to do is relax and perhaps just breathe.

As Love leaps into action,
Weaving her magic,
Organising everything
To arrange for The Miracle to be sent.

While we just hang about
Waiting.
In The Meantime
Glancing at our watches
And wondering when it will arrive.

'All in good time,' says God with a wink,
Knowing that The Miracle is *always* on its way.

48.
# WHAT IS LOVE?

So many questions about Love's Truth.

Does she Love me?
Will he stay?
Will I get my heart broken?
What is Love anyway?

Perhaps the question should be what Love is *not*?

Love is not fearful.
It is not mean.
It does not cause pain.
And it does not lie.

It does not make you question yourself;
What did I do wrong ?
Am I Loveable?
Am I worthy?

It is not adapting, changing, becoming a fantasy version of yourself.

It is not the future potential of someone that does not yet exist.

It isn't what you are not.

It is what is.
Right now.
The Truth.

Perhaps Love and Truth have something in common.
Love and Truth are both kind.
Above all else they should *always* be kind.
And if they are not
Then that is definitely *not* Love.

49.
# MY NEW BOYFRIEND

God is my boyfriend.

Have you seen us out together?
Walking down the street holding hands?

I invited him to come and live with me.
Perhaps that seems a bit sudden,
But when you know,
You *know*,
And I've been waiting for Him for a long time.

He is so kind to me.
So nurturing and loving.
He leaves me with my feet up, drinking tea,
While he sorts everything out
And makes all the decisions.

And we never argue.
If I start to lose my temper he asks me gently,
'Would you rather be right, or would you rather be
happy?'
And teaches me about Forgiveness,

Gently coaxing me back to Him every time.


God is my boyfriend and my one and only.
Perhaps that sounds like co-dependency
Or the red flag of a Love addict
Having Him as my only source of Love.


But we're happy together,
Plus it takes the pressure off everyone else,
And People Love him.


He comes with me everywhere,
Seeing the light in everyone as he shakes their hands.
He's like a local celebrity
Bringing his Holiness where ever he goes.


I think about all the special ones before Him and how
much time I wasted,
Searching for him in the wrong places.
Taking the scraps of the tiniest promise of Love.


But this time it's different.
He shows me who I really am.
He Loves me for ME,
For my Light *and* my Dark.


'There's nothing you could do that would stop me loving

you,' He tells me over and over.
And I feel safe for the first time.

I think God might be The One.

50.
# EASY PAIN

I wonder why we find pain so easy?
As humans we are wired for it,
Prepared for threat.

Of buffalo perhaps ?
Or other tribes ready to kill?

Sleeping in our caves with spears by our side,
Always on high alert.
Facing death every day.

But that was then and this is now
And we're still looking for danger.
Being wary.
Trying to protect ourselves still.

The slightest glimmer of joy and we mess it up.
The day of celebration that we spend clock watching until
it's over.
The appearance of Love and we're already planning how it
will end.

Perhaps the scientists can re-wire our brains to only
prepare for the good stuff.
Then when the bad does show up
We will be surprised,
Shocked even,
But we could deal with it when it arrives.


I would rather do that
Than live in expectation that steals so much time,
Preparing for pain
And the Death of Happiness.

51.
# MY PATIENT LOVE

I do not wish to argue with Love anymore.
I have put Him through enough,
And surely He is growing tired by now
Of trying to persuade me to open my heart
And trust His presence.

But He just remains loving and calm
When I doubt His kind words,
Or think His empathy, compassion and patience
Are surely not meant for me
But for someone else.

Someone stronger, funnier, prettier,
More sorted and whole.
Someone deserving of His affection.

Surely it is only a matter of time before He leaves me
For a person less complicated.
Less emotional.
More Loveable.
But no, He still shows up every day
Asking to let Him in.

Wanting to teach me the secret of loving me,
To show me how He sees me
Right now.
Without changing a single thing.


Oh no, I think, that's not possible.
To be Loved, surely I need to do more work on myself.
Read more books,
Go on another course,
Or get a real job and earn more money.


Or Play It Big
By stepping up,
Into The Light,
Killing my Ego
And Choosing Love
Every.
Single.
Time.
Rather than just sometimes.


Love laughs at me thinking I would need to have or be or
own or do any of those things


To get all those boxes ticked first in order to win His Love.
As if He is that shallow.

He seems mildly disgruntled and says,

'Why don't you leave it to me for now,
Since it's so easy for me.
So that all you need to do
Is allow me to Love you.'

And He does

Despite myself.
Because of myself.

## 52.
# OUR OWN REFLECTION

Looking in a mirror
Can be quite misleading.
At times traumatic,
Confronting even,
Even though it is the face we know best.

Staring at our own reflection it is as if we view ourselves
from the inside out.
Perhaps that is what repulses us so much,
Since we know the ugliness our minds are capable of
That no one else can see.

They only see beauty, strength, possibility,
Which we find laughable when our own unkindness runs
the show.

So maybe we need to look again to believe them instead,
And view ourselves as others do
Without our own distortion
Blocking us from seeing what they see.
God in the mirror.

53.
# THE FLOWER OF FORGIVENESS

The things you say to yourself in a moment of fear
Could freeze the air instantly,
And birds would fall out of the sky mid flight.

If you spoke to a rose with those words it would shrivel
and die,
And you are just as beautiful as any flower, my dear.
All of your petals are perfect,
Even those tinged with the colours of sadness, doubt,
anger.

So please promise that you will only water your roots With
raindrops of Love.
And kindness.
And Compassion.

So that you may blossom into your own forgiveness.

## 54.
# LOVE'S COURAGE

The bravest thing in the world is to continue on Love's
path.
The Fearful Ones turned away long ago,
Protecting their hearts (since Pain & Love are old friends).


But not you, oh no, you are mighty,
Staring Pain in the face,
Declaring defiantly, 'I do not care when or how you
arrive!'


Because you *know* Love,
And are unafraid of its inevitable conclusion.
So you stand tall and proud in the middle of it with
complete faith,
Despite it all with no guarantee,
No expectation, no attachment, no condition,
And in my eyes, that makes you and your Lionheart
The Most Courageous of them all.

## 55.
# MY GOD

'Do you believe in God?' you ask.
'Of course,' I say, watching you flinch.
The very word makes you uncomfortable
But do not misunderstand me.

My God is not a bearded man on a cloud,
Orchestrating earthquakes, floods and sending down
lightning bolts,
Or deciding who gets into Heaven.

Oh no, He is not up there.

Nor is he on earth, residing in churches or mosques or
religious temples,
Speaking through men at the front, talking of sin, guilt and
judgement,
Scaring us into getting down on our knees to make a deal
with their big boss.

Oh no, I do not live in fear of *my* God.

I see you're confused.
Let me explain so that you do not worry for my health any
longer.

When I say God, I only mean Love.
Although I cannot use the word 'only' when talking about
an energy so strong,
That it is indeed the most powerful force of the whole
universe.

So yes, my God is Love,
And I know it is real because I see its deepest presence
Every day in your eyes.

# ABOUT KATEY

Katey Roberts lives in Manchester and teaches Reiki, Kundalini yoga, meditation and self-empowerment courses.

She is a dedicated Connection Seeker and Truth Teller and wants people to feel less alone with their struggle of choosing Joy and Love - despite their internal MCV (Mean Chatty Voice!). Katey runs regular online poetry creative writing courses based on the method she used to write *What Love Told Me*. She is also the founder of the Connection Experiment, an online course which encourages, authenticity, belonging and community by bringing small groups together who are able to tell the truth so that we realise we are not 'the only one' who sometimes feels weird or not enough. Katey is a Tropic Ambassador- Cruelty-free, vegan natural skincare and make up (www.tropicskincare.com/pages/kateyroberts). Katey's dedication to asking 'Them Lot' for guidance, studying The Course and being a Secret Undercover Love Agent continues.

Website: www.kateyroberts.com
Facebook: Katey Roberts Holistic
Instagram: katey_love_ xx

# ACKNOWLEDGEMENTS

Gratitude to all of the Holy encounters from the past, present and future. I'm sorry. Please forgive me. Thank you. I love you.

With thanks:

To Hollie and Robert Holden, Bo, Christopher, and the Findhorn Tribe of Love Agents - The Holy Instant happened for us all that weekend - what a miracle it was! Thank you for your support, encouragement and tears. I finally realised there were too many of you to be lying !! As Bo sang to us; Hallelujah, indeed! And especially to Hollie for seeing me and officially 'witnessing' me, back in the day on a random Skype call. Thank you for giving me (and indeed all of us) permission to Be Love by simply showing up, GETTING it and telling the truth in all your glorious messy authenticity. You allow me to be myself and that is HUGE. Thank you for all your generosity. Love you.

To Nic for being My Person and never letting me question myself or your Love. You are my rock, my Biggest Love and the Darwin to my Brisbane. Thank you for always being there - even through 10 fricking years of the same story. I shall Love you until the end of time even if you despise Northerners and continue to show your pants in public. Love you.

To Spen – Thank you for your huge kindness in sharing your home, your life and your son. But especially for your generosity in Findhorn in allowing me to share the truth of our unholy Holy Relationship. I am eternally grateful to you for all of it, despite our unhappy ending. Much love and ho'oponoponos.

To Mickey for all of the pain, the Love, the lessons and kickstarting this whole journey by asking me about my Search for Love. It's going beautifully thanks. I hope yours is too. I am eternally grateful it was YOUR canal I cycled along. Thank you for all that was and never will be. Love you.

Thank you to my Big sis - Schmonkey for loving me, making me laugh and for teaching me to cycle in Holland. For coming to Perth, singing karaoke and being part of The Perfect Day by the Big Orange Rock. I'm glad I spent it with you. Thank you for also changing my life forever- the only downside to me leaving is not being in the same country anymore. Jij maakt me blij met een dode mus. Two hands on one belly. Love you.

And to my little sis, Shantellina - Thank you for showing me my shadow by shining your grace upon it. You ARE Love. Thank you for still being here. The most beautiful tribute to Elfin is that you keep waking up and showing your heart to the world every day and I am so proud of you. I thank you for showing me how to Love it all. And how to make eggs. Ik hou van je, zusje. 11:11.

To Amsterdam for showing me my shadow and being my first Home. I would not be Me without You. And for all of the Dutchies and fellow Buitenlanders for being part of it all. You will always have a place in my heart. Perhaps in another Universe we are still together and we are happy. Ik hou van je.

To Baboola and Stevo for giving me the gift of Love from day one. Thank you for accepting my weirdness and loving me anyway. I am so happy I picked you as my parents - you taught me how to Love, laugh and tell rubbish stories. Thank you for it all. Love you/SPP.

To John-boy for constantly taking the piss even though you are The Most Sensitive of Them All. I see you. Love you, Jim ps I know you are just jealous of my hair.

To PSK (Psycho Stalker Kitten) for showing me unconditional Love and being God in Cat form. You bring me joy every single day, Little Bean.

To Ma Laydees, Tribe and all the Kundaloonis, Reiki Peeps and Connection Experimentals - Thank you for all that you are, for trusting me with your hearts and for loving me despite myself.

And especially to the Nelly to my Kelly: Jayne Ashby, my Cheese-loving cheerleader who read every single blog and supported my writing from The Beginning - I know you secretly

Love me, despite the eye roll. And don't think I've forgotten that you owe me a million quid. Love you.

To Mat, the Bongo Bunglar and fellow Connection Seeker - Thank you for believing in me and banging the drums until I finally heard the beat for myself. So grateful to you for The Updates and for being my Mirror. Thank you for getting it. Love you, you Lemurian Yoga Twat.

And mainly to Lizzie; My Reiki Master and dearest friend, for your unfaltering Love, belief and support. For connecting me up in the first place. Thank you for being my not-so-silent Partner and confidante - you know it all and you manage to Love it anyway. This book would NEVER have happened without your generosity and belief in me. I am so grateful to you. You are Loved.

To Michelle, my publishing Doula for birthing this book into the world for me and making my dream come true. I am so grateful for all your patience, support and encouragement. Looking forward to reading your book soon.

To Mastin Kipp and Maui, for changing everything by seeing my Love Bug AND my sadness and allowing me to roar. I promise to take Courageous Action every day and never put a bag in an aeroplane overhead locker again because of you!

And to the 100+ of you on FB who gave me the courage to share my words. You know who you are. We get to carry each other. Love you.

And of course....thank you to A Course in Miracles for reminding me every day of my Holiness, Light and Innocence and teaching me my Function in this world. The clue is indeed in the name. And to 'Them Lot' for showing me the truth of my heart, loving me anyway and for bringing the words through me. Was nothing to do with me.

Final note:

*'Look up and see Love's Word among the stars, where She has set your Name along with Hers. Look up and find your certain destiny the world would hide but Love would have you see'*
*- ACIM*

Be Love.

Katey Roberts, 2019

Printed in Great Britain
by Amazon